...use generally contends with preservation ...detail. FXFOWLE takes a broader view. ...of architecture and planning—use, users, program, plan, circulation, structure, and sustainability, as well as facade expression and ornament—play a part in remaking historic buildings and districts. Renovations and restorations engage issues of culture, heritage, and conservation along with contemporary objectives such as identity, social engagement, and activism. Our approach reimagines and reinvents buildings for a new lifetime of use while honoring their pasts.

Sustainability inflects all aspects of adaptive reuse. When we are presented with an existing building, the question is not one of demolition but of preservation. We do not want to waste the embodied resources, whether tangible or intangible; what can be saved should be saved. The inherent strengths of any building—unique design features, passive energy conservation strategies, innovative engineering—form the backbone of the reinvented structure. Function is another key issue. A modified or entirely new program calls for a reevaluation of relationships between function and structure, plan and use. Significant changes in program often demand dramatic and creative architectural interventions.

Architectural expression is a matter of consequence in the renovations and restorations in this volume. The layering of multiple time periods—often distinguished by divergent aesthetics—requires thoughtful execution. We attempt to signal the differences between original

features and present-day insertions. Such juxtaposition calls attention to structure and details, orchestrating further evolution of a building.

The **Bronx Zoo's Lion House Reconstruction** transforms a Beaux-Arts temple structure into a sophisticated animal facility and community space, restructuring much of the original while maintaining its essence. A new immersive exhibit, *Madagascar!*, exemplifies up-to-date standards of animal care and display. The multi-purpose space is characterized by sleek modern insertions that float weightlessly within the restored historic shell.

Like the Lion House, the First Battery Armory was built in the early twentieth century. We converted the structure into corporate offices for a **Multimedia Entertainment Company**. The new program bears no relation to the initial use; we retained the historic shell while incorporating new functions in a kind of architectural puzzle. The dramatic and distinctive office highlights the dialogue between old and new.

The **Jacob K. Javits Convention Center**, built in the 1980s, aspired to advanced design and technology—design and technology beyond the capacities of the construction industry at the time. Our renovation and expansion implements cutting-edge systems that meet the potential of the original vision and also update it for the twenty-first century. Along with rehabilitating the structure, we have confronted the convention center's urban environment. Long stranded at the very edge of Manhattan, the renovation of the

Javits integrates the facility into nearby pedestrian and transportation networks.

Richardson Memorial Hall at Tulane University is a building in its second iteration of adaptive reuse. Built to house the university's School of Medicine, it was adapted for the School of Architecture in 1971. The inherent strengths of the old building, even those tailored to the medical school—open plan, natural ventilation—offer enormous potential for contemporary climate control and the programmatic needs of the architecture school. Our sustainable strategies study, incorporating a renovation and addition, reinforces the strengths of the building without compromising its historic character.

The Water Street Redevelopment Vision Plan epitomizes adaptive reuse at an urban scale. Our proposal converts a "back-of-house" service road into a dynamic new thoroughfare. Infrastructural in scope, this adaptation enacts changes that serve commercial interests and simultaneously engage the public. The new Water Street is a multiuse corridor that holds its own as a public space in New York City.

Concepts of adaptive reuse, applied in various permutations, allow program and structure to evolve. At the same time they advance larger goals of conservation and preservation within a vocabulary of modernism. The architecture of the past provides context and infrastructure in contemporary cities. Rebuilding sustainably and smartly is key to a future that safeguards resources and maintains a collective history.

The Evolution of Buildings: Repositioning and Adaptive Reuse

Kenneth Schwartz

Kenneth Schwartz, FAIA is the Dean and Favrot Professor of Architecture at the Tulane School of Architecture.

Architecture, landscape, and urban planning are not static fields. These disciplines of the built and natural environments play a part in an interconnected, interdisciplinary world and are subject to its ebbs and flows, its evolutions and adaptations. Architectural work must be situated within the warp and weft of a holistic fabric and must connect the present with the past in particular ways. The same may be said of music, literature, painting, and certain other modes of creative expression; these tap into the implications of received tradition and authenticity implied by a human production that is carefully calibrated with respect to materials, methods of fabrication, and expression in final form. However, buildings, landscapes, and cities, and especially the adaptive reuse of existing buildings, offer something further: a meaningful opportunity to explore the dynamic tensions between old and new, between background and foreground, and between accumulated strengths derived through interconnectivity.

Physicality

FXFOWLE has produced a number of compelling projects that deliberately tease out the inherent qualities of historic structures while introducing decidedly contemporary ambitions for high levels of performance in sustainable design and energy consumption. The renovation of Warren Hall at Cornell University and the Richardson Memorial Hall Sustainable Strategies Study at Tulane University are two impressive examples. In both cases, the architects examined hundred-year-old buildings, identifying their innate qualities to provide the structural grounding for subsequent adaptations. The conception of each project involves a careful balance between old and new, a balance that is mutually reinforcing rather than a simplistic dichotomy. Tying together new and old within each project integrates and blurs distinctions, imparting to each structure a memorable strength that will last for the next 100 years.

Sustainability

The concept of adaptive reuse is not new. Structures that have been built to last have always evolved, avoiding obsolescence in their lifetimes. The value of adaptive reuse has been recognized beyond traditional preservation quarters only in recent decades. As global climate change and the impact of energy use have become more thoroughly considered, a convergence of interests has led to greater acceptance of restoration as a compelling strategy. From the standpoint of embodied energy to the potential of mining environmental intelligence from past periods, many institutional and civic buildings present unusually rich opportunities for rehabilitation. These structures may reap benefits from a contemporary engagement with new uses while maintaining continuity with hidden infrastructure aspects. One of the ironic results of a careful approach to the adaptive reuse of existing buildings is that, in the most successful cases, the author's signature can almost entirely disappear. While some architects weave their expressions into a historic fabric in assertive ways (Carlo Scarpa at the Castelvecchio in Verona is a powerful example), others consciously eschew such authorial imprint. FXFOWLE has most often chosen a quiet and self-effacing approach, which, in another irony, requires a great deal of effort, finesse, and restraint. The work of the office is as much about repairing as it is about creating a new condition from a completely new set of circumstances.

Tectonics

Building systems and approaches to passive versus active aspects play an important role in FXFOWLE's operations on these designs. For example, on the Richardson Memorial Hall project, the firm and their consultants explore the total transformation of building systems in a manner that challenges assumptions about the extent to which passive strategies can be utilized to reduce the demands on active means. This agenda is particularly challenging in a hot and humid climate. Even at the early stage of a feasibility study, energy modeling and the associated consideration of various passive design approaches led to identifying methods that would minimize the visual impact of contemporary technologies in the adapted historic structure. To deliberately mitigate the damaged historic conditions that evolved in the energy-intensive, post–World War II decades, the team proposed removing almost all postwar additions.

Cultural and Symbolic Value

The adaptations in this volume demonstrate a connection to the history of a building, to contemporary conditions, and to future evolutions. All respect and maintain the collective memory embedded within the human experience of the structure. The renovation of Warren Hall, one of the original structures on the Agricultural Quadrangle, reinforces the continued narrative of useful knowledge in this land-grant component

of the Cornell campus. With Richardson Memorial Hall, the sustainability study acknowledges the building's origins, providing a link to its original and dominant use throughout most of the twentieth century: the original home of the Tulane School of Medicine.

Discipline and Production

Creating effective sustainable projects demands a set of relationships across a number of disciplines, particularly architecture, engineering, and landscape architecture. Whether these relationships form around concepts of integrated project delivery or operate in more traditional iterative modes of collaboration, they always depend on mutual recognition of shared dependency around specialized knowledge and generalized interest. This form of inter-connectivity, unlike more hierarchical models of practice, is especially rich when it involves a simultaneous interest in preserving buildings with rich histories and in engaging ambitious sustainable agendas.

The work of FXFOWLE is exemplary. By building with respect, authenticity, and inter-connectivity, the office contributes to a more sustainable and humane future, carefully crafted across time. The firm has been a national leader in repositioning the profession with thoughtful attention to the value of continuity in adaptive reuse of structures and landscapes. In process and in production, FXFOWLE demonstrates the powerful principles of sustainable practice.

When working with a historic building, that building becomes the context. The program, systems, technologies, and architectural language must "fit" and leverage the context. The new architecture for the Lion House resulted from a creative dialogue with the rich character of the original Beaux-Arts structure. Sylvia Smith

Designated a New York City Landmark in 1992, the Lion House at the Bronx Zoo is the largest building on Astor Court, an assemblage of Beaux-Arts buildings designed by Heins & LaFarge. The six brick, limestone, and terra-cotta buildings, constructed between 1899 and 1910, define the courtyard, the symbolic heart of the zoo campus. The Lion House is distinguished by symmetry, elegant monumentality, a refined yet bold material palette, and rich articulation.

Despite its architectural significance, the building no longer functioned as a modern animal facility. When it was completed in 1903, the Lion House was considered state-of-the-art: the big cats were housed in large rooms, not small cages, and could move between exterior and interior. Instead of bars, a fine, almost invisible mesh covered the exterior enclosures. Visitors viewed the animals from an expansive hall or from the courtyard promenade. Over time, this model became outmoded, and in the late 1970s, the big cats were moved to spacious, more naturalistic outdoor environments. The Lion House stood empty for more than twenty-five years.

Our work at the Lion House was not a restoration project. We had to deconstruct and then reconstruct major portions of the building to transform the outdated facility into something new: an immersive exhibit, *Madagascar!*, its associated support areas, and a gracious community room. The intervention preserves the historic character of the Lion House but updates it for twenty-first-century objectives—habitat-sensitive animal exhibition, flexible public accommodation, and efficient infrastructure for water, air, and electricity. Additionally, the project serves as a model for the sensitive and sustainable adaptation of historic buildings.

We started by enlarging the available volume, both physically and conceptually. The landmarked building exterior was sacrosanct; in order to create space where none existed, we excavated. The footprint of the cellar has been more than doubled; the height of this level is now eleven feet instead of seven. Some of this additional volume is devoted to *Madagascar!*; the extra height creates a contoured site more reminiscent of the habitats of the island nation. The rest of the cellar is devoted to animal care, life support and mechanical systems, and back-of-house areas for the community space. The expansion of the lower level was an extremely delicate operation. The historic building was essentially levitated, supported by structured shoring; while the excavation was under way, interior elements were cataloged and removed for reinstallation or reuse in other areas.

Complementing the exhibit is a flexible community room. We converted the former viewing hall into a multipurpose space that both maintains and modernizes the historic character of the building. Inserted within the hall is a glass, stainless-steel, and limestone pavilion that juxtaposes past and present. This two-story floating "jewel box" accommodates restrooms on the first floor and a high-tech conference room above. The materials and their expression echo the industrial character of the hall's original cast-iron trusses.

The west terrace, formerly a utilitarian enclosure, has been transformed into a semi-private outdoor extension of the community space. New doors inserted into existing Palladian window surrounds provide access to the terrace. The sentry lions that once "guarded" the building entry have been moved to a position of honor on axis with these new doors.

New infrastructure in the Lion House supports *Madagascar!* as well as the adjacent sea lion pool. The new systems are small and efficient, reducing use of energy and space alike. High-tech water filtration eliminates the need to purge the sea lion tank, saving thousands of gallons of water. A geothermal heat-pump system heats and cools the building; cooling towers are not required. Ductwork, fans, and other climate-control mechanisms have been downsized as much as possible. We replaced the original glass skylights with ethylene tetrafluoroethylene units. Composed of layers of mylar, these units may be inflated or deflated to control transmission of natural light and heat.

Ventilation and structure hide in plain sight. Columns and ductwork double as trees in the exhibit. The pergola ceiling that defines the pathway through the exhibit limits views of the infrastructure above. In the multipurpose space, a raised-floor displacement system delivers heating and cooling, eliminating ductwork that would have obscured the cast-iron trusses. Sprinklers are integrated into an acoustical-panel and wood-batten ceiling system that re-creates the character of the original ceiling.

The Lion House reflects a singular attitude toward preservation and modernization. The outer building form appears unchanged, and building systems are largely invisible. Functional historic elements, such as the entry doors, are restored; components where the use has changed, such as the cage enclosures, are reinterpreted. New insertions are plainly inspired by the logical construction and rich palette of the original architecture. The DNA of the Beaux-Arts landmark guided us as we accommodated the animals, plants, and people who occupy the Lion House. Old is new again.

Viewing Hall, 1903

1903 Structure

Cage Enclosure Removed

Steel Beams Installed
at Column Line B
Wall Below Removed

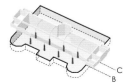

Existing Structure Shored
Cellar Excavated
Footprint Expanded
Column Lines B and C
and Foundation Extended
New Cellar Slab Poured

New Floors and
Terrace Slab Poured

New Cage Enclosure Walls
New Interior Walls
Conference Room Insertion

New Roof Structure with
High-Performance Skylights

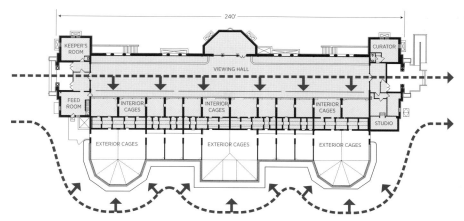

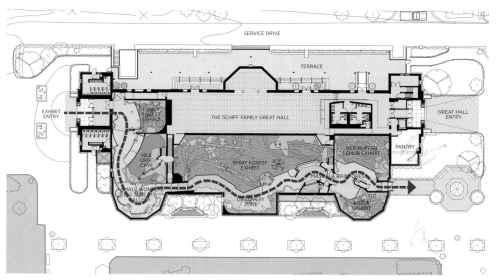

Historic First Floor Plan and Visitor Path

First Floor Plan and Visitor Path

Construction: November 2005

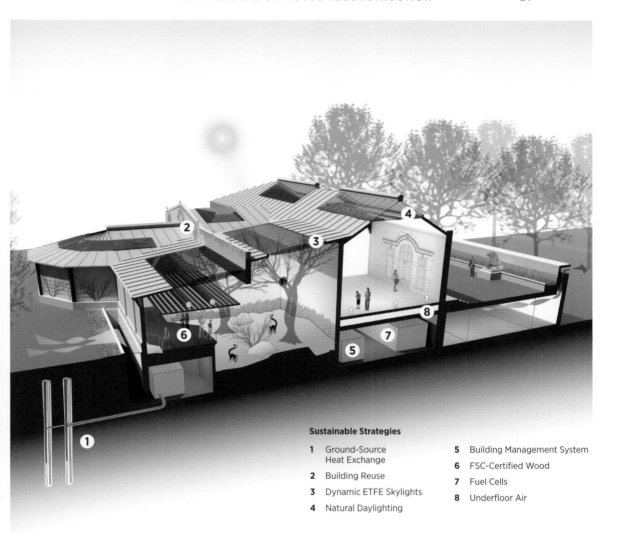

Sustainable Strategies

1   Ground-Source
    Heat Exchange

2   Building Reuse

3   Dynamic ETFE Skylights

4   Natural Daylighting

5   Building Management System

6   FSC-Certified Wood

7   Fuel Cells

8   Underfloor Air

RICHARDSON MEMORIAL HALL SUSTAINABILITY STUDY
NEW ORLEANS, LOUISIANA, 2011
TULANE UNIVERSITY
67,500 SQUARE FEET, LEED PLATINUM (ANTICIPATED)

Originally built for the School of Medicine in 1908, Richardson Memorial Hall was heavily dependent on natural ventilation. Over time, these and other sustainable characteristics were abandoned and replaced with multiple mechanical systems. Our task was to return the building to its roots, and to rediscover the role of natural systems in the building's operations.
Guy Geier

Tulane's Richardson Memorial Hall, home to the University's School of Medicine since the early twentieth century, was transformed into the School of Architecture in 1971. Our early-twenty-first-century study of the building, which focused on sustainable strategies, subjects Richardson to transformation for a second time. The proposed renovation assesses the ongoing needs of architecture students in the context of a program that includes sustainability as a core component. New techniques for digital design and fabrication and the incorporation of information technology networks and working methodologies are also important disciplines for this generation of students. While our work began by addressing deficiencies in the operations and mechanical systems, it grew into a more comprehensive evaluation of and strategy for the future of the historic building.

The Tulane School of Architecture focuses on collaborative community outreach under the philosophy that awareness and engagement backed by tangible acts can transform both students and the community. Students are trained to work together and to understand and embrace the rapidly evolving profession of architecture. Our renovation capitalizes on synergies between the philosophy and pedagogy of the school on the one hand and Richardson Memorial Hall on the other. It will position the school at the forefront of campus sustainability initiatives and transform the building into a learning environment that both teaches and embodies principles of sustainability.

We started with a series of charrettes with students and other members of the Tulane architecture community. Among the objectives that emerged were upgrading the building envelope in terms of sustainability; improving all mechanical, electrical, plumbing, and fire-protection systems; addressing building code deficiencies; minimizing noise disturbance from an adjacent chiller plant facility; and enhancing information technology. Also included were upgrades to the physical plant: more spaces for informal collaboration; better campus connections; expanded fabrication shop facilities; and more comfortable faculty offices. Finally, it was vital that the historic structure could be integrated into the curriculum as a teaching tool in itself.

Richardson Memorial Hall was built, coincidentally, in the Richardsonian Romanesque style. Its generous proportions and large floor-through open spaces offered generous laboratories for the medical school. Constructed before the widespread use of electric light and mechanical ventilation, the building was designed with many inherent sustainable strategies. More than 250 windows and a central tower that acted as a heat chimney provided ample daylight and cross-ventilation. The large, daylight-flooded rooms were equally suitable for studio space once the School of Architecture moved in. But over the years the building was altered, and newly invented mechanical and environmental control systems were added to the building in a scattershot manner.

Our approach focused on rediscovering the intrinsic sustainability of Richardson Hall, on reinventing the natural systems that once determined building mechanics. It also incorporated recommendations for energy efficiency, water management, ecological materials, indoor environmental comfort, and maintenance and operations. New mechanical systems take advantage of natural ventilation as much as possible but utilize heating and air conditioning when necessary. The design reveals this mixed-mode system on a dashboard so that students can see and explore the sustainable mechanics, the historic fabric, and the interface between the two.

The arrangement of major interior spaces has been reconfigured to serve both practical ends and sustainable goals. A large multipurpose lecture and reception room occupies a prominent location relative to the overall campus; administration offices are located near the main entry, in what was their original position. A commons overlooks the fabrication shop, which in turn gives way to a new courtyard where students can construct and display temporary work. A café on the ground floor connects to an exterior terrace, improving connections between the building and campus, and an outdoor classroom, seating, and bike racks further invite the campus to engage with the school.

A long, thin addition to the east of the building solves functional challenges and provides critical new infrastructure. Faculty offices (formerly on the ground floor of Richardson) are more convenient to studios, improving access and communication. Meeting rooms and pin-up spaces supplement design studios. Fire stairs at each end of the addition bring the building up to code. The new construction also enhances the natural ventilation, drawing hot air up and out through a gap between the historic building and the addition.

The western facade of the building, which faces historic Gibson Quad, presents a challenge: it is the most subject to solar gain but the least flexible because of its importance as a historic facade. To minimize the effect of direct sunlight without significantly altering the facade, we have proposed an internal shade. In time, we will work with the students of the School of Architecture to develop a demountable external shading system. Fabricated in the Tulane shop, this system could be developed into a commercial product for other historic structures.

Historic Lecture Hall

Historic Nursing Lab

Existing Student Workspace

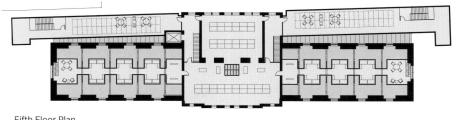

Fifth Floor Plan

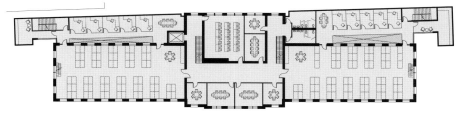

Fourth Floor Plan

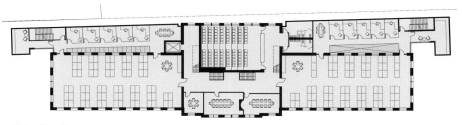

Third Floor Plan

Second Floor Plan

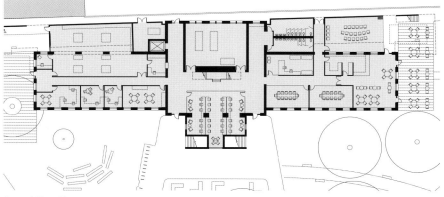

Ground Floor Plan

Student Workshops

Main Entry

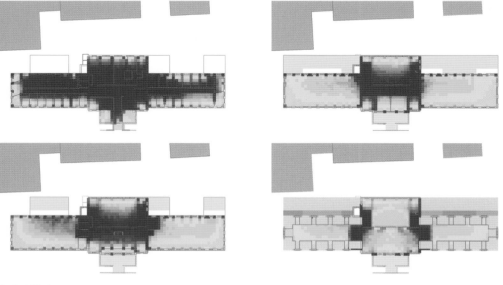

Ecotect Study

Daylight Autonomy
>100
<100
<92
<83
<75
<67
<58
<50
<42
<33
<25
<17
<8
<0

Sustainable Strategies

1   Building Reuse
2   Rainwater Harvesting
3   Daylight Harvesting
4   Photovoltaic and Solar
    Thermal Panels
5   Habitable Green Roof
    and Wall
6   Chilled Beams
7   Natural Ventilation
8   Ceiling Fans
9   Rain Garden/
    Stormwater Retention

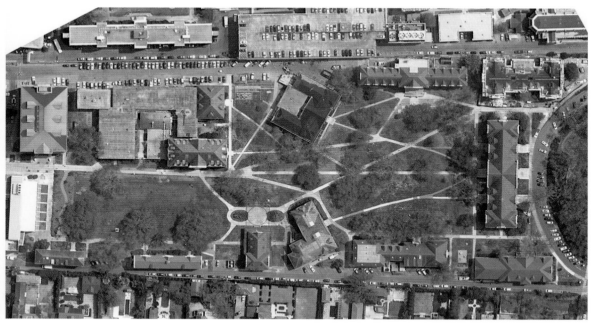

Aerial Photograph of "Front Campus"

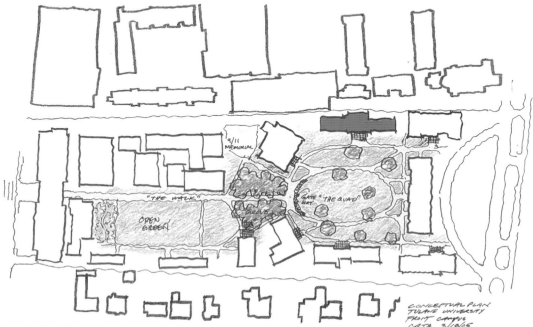

Concept Plan for "Front Campus" March 2005

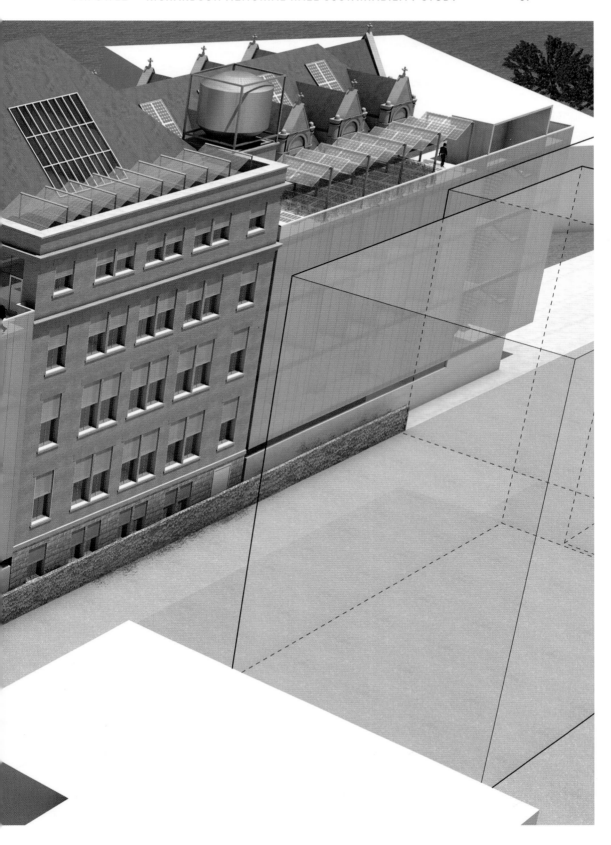

This project consists of a modern insertion into a historic fabric. The two elements coexist in a dialogue; neither drowns the other out. The modern additions are unified with clean and polished materials that play against the original framework. Guy Geier

Located on Manhattan's Upper West Side, one block from Central Park, the First Battery Armory was constructed in 1901–3 by Horgan and Slattery Architects for the New York City Armory Board. In 1913, the First Battery relocated, and between 1913 and 1976, the building was renovated multiple times for various tenants. In 1977, the building was remodeled by a television network for use as a studio. Window openings were filled with brick, a pipe grid was installed in the ceiling, and large ducts, visible from the street, were positioned on the roof.

In 2012, we converted the three-story stone and brick building—a linear head house along the street with a drill hall behind—into the corporate offices for a multimedia entertainment company. The armory is listed on the National Register of Historic Places, and our design restores the shell as rigorously as possible. The interior is reconfigured and modernized but preserves the expression of the volume of the drill hall and the feel of the early-twentieth-century building, including its original brick walls. Modern and antique elements are differentiated by means of materiality. Historic portions of the building have been restored with original components (brick and trusses), fabricated to match what exists (light fixtures), or updated to meet code requirements in a way that references the past (roof structure). All historic steel—ceiling trusses, handrails, building details—is painted gray, fostering a unified industrial look and establishing an internal dialogue. Materials for the modern insertions create a clear contrast.

The interior of the head house accommodates private offices. Two new mezzanines in the drill hall provide efficient work and meeting areas. At the juncture between the head house and the drill hall, we inserted a light slot. Skylights cast natural light into this circulation zone of stairs and elevators. On the far side of the drill hall, opposite the light slot, zoning regulations restricted construction to a single floor. Within this unusual thirty-foot-wide space, we developed a flexible area for presentations, events, and sales meetings. This communal zone is an internal landscape that offers visual interest without actual views to the exterior.

The new stair in the light slot serves as a social space; stretching diagonally, it conducts light through the building, all the way to the basement. At each end of the light slot is a conference room that overlooks the office interior. The mezzanine work space supports a flexible work environment. Glass partitions increase visual transparency and allow light to filter through to offices, workstations, and conference rooms. Mezzanine floors are flat-slab construction; their smooth, polished finish contrasts with the rough texture of the old brick walls. In the basement offices, indirect illumination reveals the historic flat-arch ceiling.

Construction took into account the nature of the building as well as the requirements of historic preservation.

We gutted and stripped the building, then rebuilt it piece by piece with what was salvageable. We restored and painted the roof trusses and added a new roof structure inspired by other armories of the period. An acoustic perforated-metal ceiling references the tongue-and-groove boards that were used originally. We restored two rows of skylights over the light slot but redesigned them to avoid excessive heat gain.

Building systems acknowledge contemporary standards for sustainability and energy conservation. Efficient mechanical systems, such as underfloor air distribution, conserve energy and maintain indoor air quality. Daylight and occupancy sensors also keep energy usage low. All mechanical equipment is accommodated within the building but out of view.

Alterations to the exterior were subject to the approval of the Landmarks Preservation Commission. At the entryway, we designed light fixtures inspired by old photographs and restored the look of the original double-leaf barn doors. Within these door openings we developed a contemporary entrance of aluminum-and-glass doors, which allow visual access from the street into the building. The doors are a metaphor for our work at the armory—a contemporary insertion that reinforces the architecture of a historic building.

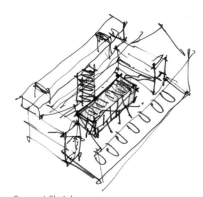

Concept Sketch

Historic Drill Hall, 1913

Sound Stage, 2009

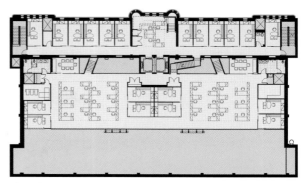

Third Floor Plan

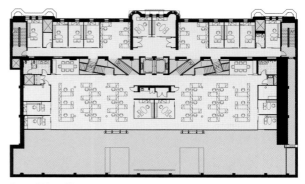

Second Floor Plan

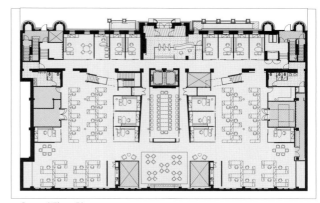

Ground Floor Plan

Basement Plan

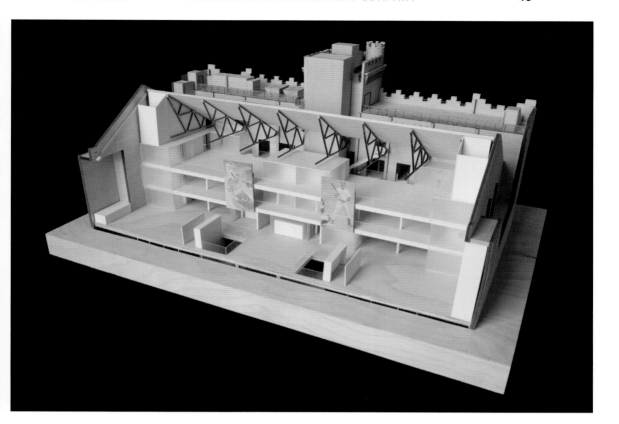

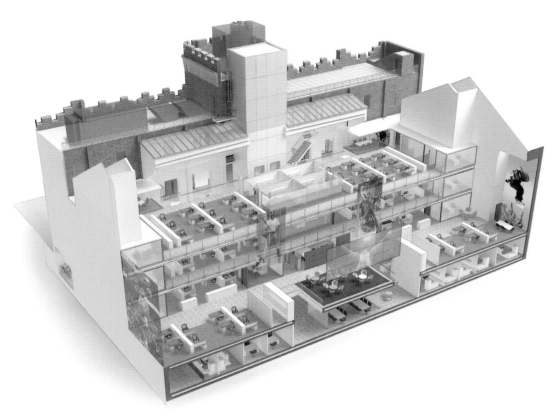

The original building was ahead of its time technologically—the space frame was cutting-edge—but it was fraught with problems and undermined by unforeseen budget constraints. Our goal was to retain the integrity and vision of the original design while capitalizing on opportunities to reinvent, revitalize, and sustain this dynamic, world-class facility.
Bruce Fowle

Located on four city blocks on the far west side of Manhattan, the Javits Center is New York City's primary venue for trade shows and conventions. A megastructure designed in 1979 by I. M. Pei and Partners, it was conceived as a new incarnation of Joseph Paxton's 1851 Crystal Palace in London. The building makes use of a space frame, or lightweight structural system of interconnected trusses. But while the vision for the building was advanced—the space frame is the largest in the world—the necessary material technology, funding, and political will were lacking. Instead of fulfilling its promise as the next Crystal Palace, the Javits Center was quickly maligned by both the public and building users.

Our work on the Javits Center restored its technological promise and overhauled its environmental and quality-of-life impact. The project includes a complete renovation and modernization, a northward expansion, and a comprehensive sustainability strategy. The building's appearance, systems, urban linkages, and day-to-day performance have been transformed; the original space frame and overall functionality maintained.

The original design vision of the Javits Center was seriously compromised during its implementation. One bay of exposition space, about 60,000-square-feet, was eliminated. The 185-foot-high main entrance—the contemporary Crystal Palace—was never truly crystalline, since the only glass that met the performance standards of the day was dark and gloomy. The interior was overcome by commercial kiosks, signs, and trade fair trappings. Even the location of the building worked against it—the site was isolated along the Hudson River's derelict piers and was unconnected to the metropolis at street level or via the subway system. Our work had to focus not only on the convention center but on its place within the city, notably its relationship to burgeoning neighborhoods and new waterfront promenades nearby.

The Javits is not a structure that lends itself to easy modification—components are either cast concrete or supported by the unalterable space frame. We had to find innovative solutions to design concerns as well as creative approaches to public building processes and approvals. State and city sustainability requirements aligned with our efforts to reduce energy consumption by more than 26 percent. The renovated interior spaces have considerably more natural light, better indoor air quality, operational efficiency, and adaptability.

A new high-performance curtain wall simplifies and lightens the aesthetics of the original facade. The change from five-by-five-foot to five-by-ten-foot glass modules with minimal mullions creates an airy and open appearance. Advanced coatings, frit patterns, and thermal breaks in the support system enhance thermal performance. Clear glass, reduced reflectivity, and fewer framing members afford more transparency. We devoted much study to transmitting more light with less glare, improving interior ambience. In addition, the frit pattern and lesser reflectivity of the glass created a visual barrier to migrating birds. Formerly the Javits Center had been rated the deadliest building for bird collisions in New York; working with ornithologists and guided by recent research, we mitigated the bird mortality rate by more than 90 percent.

A stainless-steel panel system replaces about a third of the opaque spandrel glass of the original facade, modernizing the appearance of the structure and increasing performance. A 6.7-acre green roof—the building's fifth facade—is as cost-effective as a conventional roof, mitigates the heat-island effect of the building as well as temperatures in the area, helps protect the roof membrane, and reduces stormwater runoff by an average of 40 percent. A new retractable gantry system facilitates cleaning the glass skylights and walls.

The redesign of the interior focused on upgrading organization and efficiency, as well as occupant comfort. The more transparent curtain wall, less opaque skylight systems, and light gray paint on the space frame have dramatically transformed the voluminous public spaces. Lighting fixtures are more efficient and produce a brighter, more comfortable tonality. New mechanical systems have improved the indoor air quality, reduced ambient noise, and significantly saved on energy consumption. Visitor entries have been consolidated into a series of distinct portals. Commercial kiosks and food services have been merged into orderly structures. Gantries, catwalk access, and banner drops ease show installation and interior maintenance. The diamond-patterned terrazzo of the original floor has been replaced with soft tones of gray terrazzo; stripes on the concourse level extend to an exterior plaza, emphasizing the relationship between interior and exterior.

An evolution in planning in New York City aided our efforts to integrate the Javits into its surroundings. Hudson River Park, on the west side of the convention center, and the proposed Hudson Park and Boulevard, part of the multiblock Hudson Yards development to the south and east, are expanding the surrounding public realm to the waterfront and into the city. The 7 subway line is being extended to the Javits, greatly improving access to the site. The diaphanous curtain wall strengthens view corridors along east-west streets and reveals the remade convention center to conference attendees and neighborhood residents alike. We reconceptualized the vehicular drop-off area as a public plaza with outdoor seating, retail kiosks, and plantings; it is a vital link between the city and Hudson River Park. A future pull-off lane on 11th Avenue will draw trucks, buses, and taxis away from the plaza, enriching the streetscape and creating a better and safer arrival experience for all visitors. Approach to, prospect upon, experience within, and view from the building: all contribute to a revitalized, reinvigorated Javits Center that finally lives up to its potential.

Original Curtain Wall

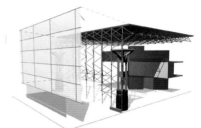

Renovation Plan

New Curtain Wall

Concept Rendering by I. M. Pei & Associates, 1979

Exterior Pre-Renovation

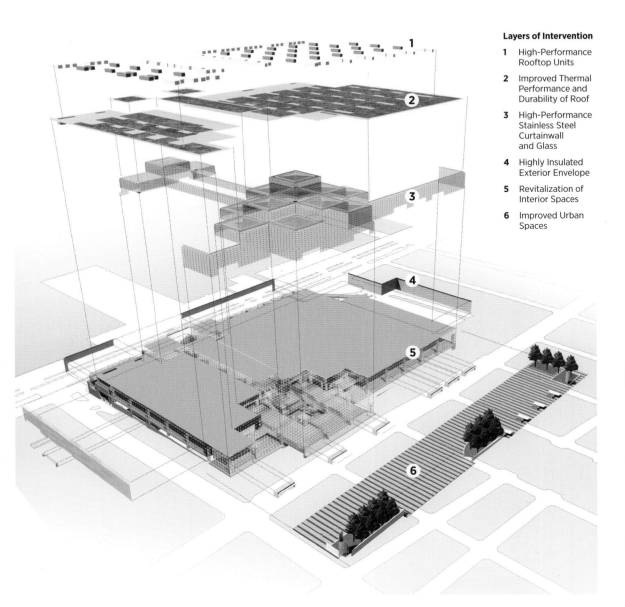

Layers of Intervention

1   High-Performance Rooftop Units

2   Improved Thermal Performance and Durability of Roof

3   High-Performance Stainless Steel Curtainwall and Glass

4   Highly Insulated Exterior Envelope

5   Revitalization of Interior Spaces

6   Improved Urban Spaces

Crystal Palace Pre-Renovation

Construction: Glass Replacement

Before: Galleria

After: Galleria

Before: River Pavilion

After: River Pavilion

Aerial Photograph Pre-Renovation

Construction: Green Roof

Green Roof, Completed Phase 1

Water Street was designed in the early 1960s as the service backbone for an efficient office district. But as an urban roadway it failed to engage the public at the street level. Our plan promotes a more attractive, 24/7 environment. Although these strategies have been developed specifically for Water Street, they can be applied to any environment where pedestrian activity at the street lacks energy. Mark Strauss

Originally a warehouse district for the old port of New York, Water Street runs from the Battery to South Street Seaport. The area was redefined in the 1960s as an office precinct for the banking and insurance industries. In the early twenty-first century, as former office buildings are converted to residential towers and the financial district has become a tourist destination, Water Street lacks the vitality of the city's other commercial corridors. Our study of Water Street remakes the avenue for a new generation, promoting mixed uses and strengthening connections to adjacent neighborhoods.

The primary problems with Water Street are its width—four lanes of traffic in two directions, plus two lanes of parking—and its character—few amenities or retail options. Additionally, numerous privately owned public spaces pull activity away from the public area of the street. The new plan offers a more dynamic, pedestrian-friendly setting; appealing multiuse areas; an engagement with the public realm; and innovative programming. Our study identified four guiding principles: rescale Water Street to create an iconic boulevard; strengthen the connections to both the historic fabric of the area and the waterfront; realign public and ground-floor spaces to animate street life; and extend the hours of activity in the district. The emphasis is on the future, but the plan acknowledges the history of the street and of the area.

A key recommendation of the study was to reduce the vehicular right-of-way on Water Street from 60 to 42 feet. A planted median, bike lane, and bump-outs replace two lanes of traffic, simultaneously adding landscape and promoting pedestrian safety. In addition, the sidewalk on the west side of Water Street is extended by six feet; along with another four feet annexed from the existing sidewalk, this new ten-foot amenity strip offers café seating, kiosks, bus shelters, and clusters of trees. On the east side of the roadway, a five-foot strip supports a single row of trees. At the entrance points to the area—Whitehall Street to the south and Fulton Street to the north—are gateways with plazas, landscaping, and public art; lighting schemes also draw attention to the Water Street corridor. Sustainability has been designed into hardscape and softscape alike. Generous bioswales will mitigate and filter stormwater runoff, and street trees will provide shade and improved air quality. Drought-tolerant, indigenous plantings will support bird and insect habitat, and light-colored materials will reduce the heat-island effect.

Few visual cues reveal that Water Street is just two blocks away from the East River. For decades a forbidding zone, the riverfront has gradually been reopened to public use. Improving the streets and connecting Water Street and the East River will draw pedestrians from the waterfront to the city and from the city to the waterfront. Our proposal for Mannahatta Park, which links Wall Street to the East River, expands the green space into a more significant center of activity. A flexible gathering and event area, as well as a gateway from Wall Street, Mannahatta Park supports both regular uses, such as an outdoor market, and singular occasions, like outdoor dancing and performances.

The privately owned public spaces along Water Street are perhaps the biggest challenge in remaking the area. Between the 1960s and 1980s, these plazas and arcades were built as "bonuses" under the 1961 zoning code. However, most of them are not well-designed and do not meet current standards for public space. Further, there are too many of the featureless expanses—eight acres in total—making the street feel emptier than it actually is.

Our proposal recommends upgrading the public spaces that already have good access to sunlight and strong connections to the East River; enclosing large arcades and building over underused plazas; converting blank walls into animated facades with vegetation, responsive lighting, and display; and encouraging activity with art, landscape, lighting, and kiosks. Such attractions as art installations and lighting enhancements require no adjustments to zoning; more substantial refurbishments—building over plazas, inserting retail and other amenities, creating large swaths of landscape—would require regulatory change.

The final components in the Water Street study are not urban or architectural but programmatic. While physical changes set the stage for a vastly improved public realm, it is events and innovations that will draw workers, local residents, and visitors to the area. A coordinated framework for exhibitions, performances, and other entertainments will transform Water Street, fostering a vibrant and engaging environment, building a meaningful connection to people and place, and extending activity well into the evening, through the weekend, and across the seasons.

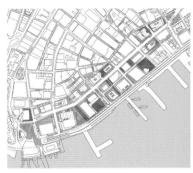

■ Infill of Arcades and POPS (Privately Owned Public Spaces)   ■ Parks   ■ POPS

■ Parks   ■ POPS   ■ Infill of Arcades and POPS   ✱ Active/Program   ⋯⋯ Programming Connections   —⋅— East/West Connections

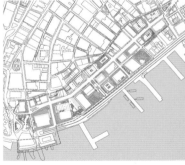

■ Plazas   Arcades

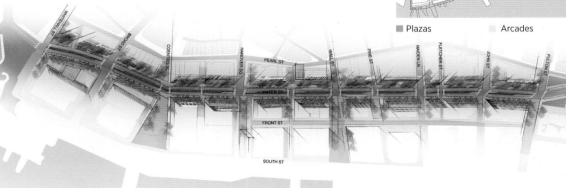

Master Plan

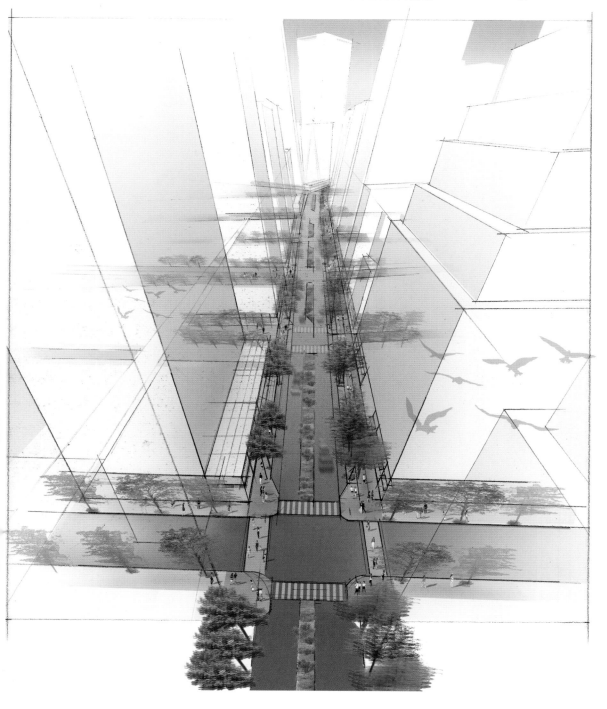

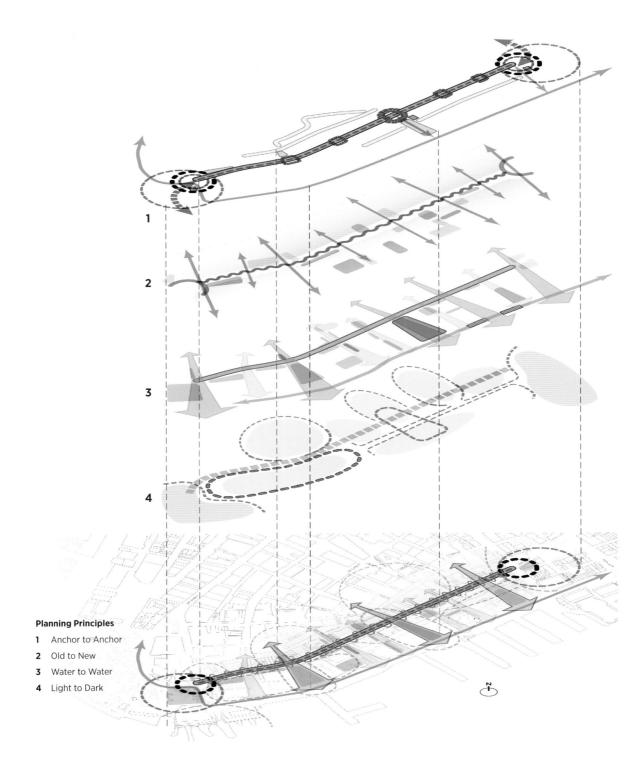

Planning Principles

1   Anchor to Anchor
2   Old to New
3   Water to Water
4   Light to Dark

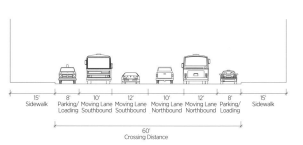

15' Sidewalk | 8' Parking/ Loading | 10' Moving Lane Southbound | 12' Moving Lane Southbound | 10' Moving Lane Northbound | 12' Moving Lane Northbound | 8' Parking/ Loading | 15' Sidewalk

60' Crossing Distance

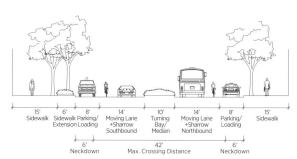

15' Sidewalk | 6' Sidewalk Extension | 8' Parking/ Loading | 14' Moving Lane +Sharrow Southbound | 10' Turning Bay/ Median | 14' Moving Lane +Sharrow Northbound | 8' Parking/ Loading | 15' Sidewalk

6' Neckdown | 42' Max. Crossing Distance | 6' Neckdown

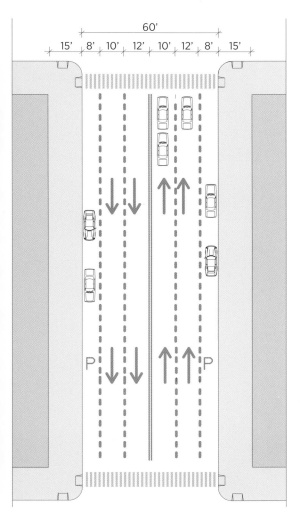

Existing Street Configuration

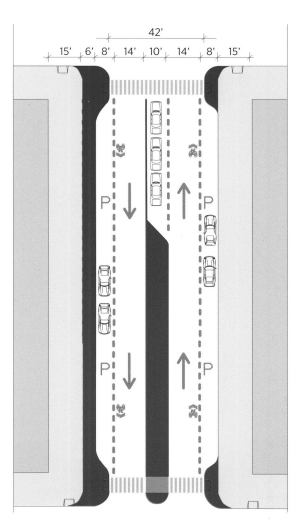

Proposed Street Configuration

Before

After

Before

After

Senior Partners
Gerard F. X. Geier II, FAIA, FIIDA, LEED
Sudhir S. Jambhekar, FAIA, RIBA, LEED
Daniel J. Kaplan, FAIA, LEED
Sylvia J. Smith, FAIA, LEED
Mark E. Strauss, FAIA, AICP/PP, LEED

Partners
Heidi L. Blau, FAIA, LEED
Tim Milam, AIA, LEED
John Schuyler, AIA, LEED

Founding Principal
Bruce S. Fowle, FAIA, LEED

Project Credits

Introduction/The Evolution of Buildings

Bronx Zoo's Lion House Reconstruction,
David Sundberg/Esto (p2, 10),
FXFOWLE (p8)
Jacob K. Javits Convention Center
Renovation, David Sundberg/Esto
(p4, 12)
Multimedia Entertainment Company,
Frank Oudeman (p6, 14)

Bronx Zoo's Lion House Reconstruction

Partner-in-Charge: Sylvia Smith
Project Manager: Susan Masi
Project Architect: Tom Fox
Project Designer: Frank D. MacNelly
Team: Nicholas Hollot, Paul Kim,
Heng-Choong Leong, Daniel McKee,
Scott Melching, Sean Murphy, Peter
Pesce, Krishna Rao, Alexander Redfern,
Mark Rusitzky, Timothy Sudweeks,
Jacquelyn Suozzi, Katherine Sutton,
Conrad Talley, Paul Tapogna, Nicholas
Tocheff, Andrew Varela, Raquel Vasallo

Structural Engineer: Anastos
Engineering Associates
MEP Engineer: Kallen & Lemelson
Consulting Engineers
Vertical Transportation: VDA Associates
Acoustical: Cerami & Associates Inc.
Lighting: Hayden McKay Lighting
Design Inc.
Landscape: Quennel Rothschild &
Partners LLP
A/V: DVI Communications, Inc.
Site, Civil, Geotechnical: Langan
Engineering, Environmental, Surveying
and Landscape Architecture, D.P.C.
Preservation: Building
Conservation Associates, Inc
Food Facility: Romano Gatland
Cost Estimating: Wolf and Company
LEED Consulting: Viridian
Energy & Environmental, LLC

Photography: David Sundberg/Esto,
historic photography courtesy
of Wildlife Conservation Society

Richardson Memorial Hall Sustainable Strategies Study

Partner-in-Charge: Guy Geier
Project Manager: Peter Pesce
Team: Bob Cuk, Ilana Judah

Associate Architect: el dorado inc
MEP Engineer: Altieri Sebor Wieber LLC
Climate Engineer: Trans Solar
Structural Engineer, Building Envelope,
Preservation Technology:
Simpson Gumpertz & Heger
Landscape Architect:
Andropogon Landscape Design
Cost Estimating: Faithful + Gould
Photography: workshop images
by David Armentor, historic images
courtesy of Tulane School of Architecture

Multimedia Entertainment Company

Partner-in-Charge: Guy Geier
Project Manager: Michael Syracuse
Project Architect: Erica Godun
Project Designer: Daniel Jacoby
Team: Gregory Chann, Violette de la
Selle, Erica Godun, Sylvia Hernandez,
Ervin Hirsan, Illiana Ivanova,
Ilana Judah, Heng-Choong Leong,
Robert Loken, Alvaro Quintana,
Krishna Rao, Gerard Sambets Jr.,
Stephanie Schreiber

Structural Engineer:
Anastos Engineering Associates
MEP Engineer: Dagher Engineering
Civil, Geotechnical Engineer: Langan
Engineering, Environmental, Surveying
and Landscape Architecture, D.P.C.

Lighting: Brandston Partnership Inc.
Vertical Circulation: Van Deusen
& Associates
Acoustic: Cerami and Associates Inc.
Landmarks, Preservation: Building
Conservation Associates, Inc.
Code, Expeditor: Design 2147 Limited
Construction Manager:
Skanska USA Building Inc.
Photography: Frank Oudeman,
historic images courtesy of New York
State Military Museum

Jacob K. Javits Convention Center Renovation

Partner-in-Charge: Bruce Fowle,
Daniel Kaplan
Project Director: Nicolas Ryan,
John Adams Dix*
Project Manager: Larry Dalziel*
Project Architects: Jason Abbey,
Michael Buesing, Kimberly Garcia,
Peter Olney, Cory Goings
Team: Vincent Gentile*, Kazuhiro
Adachi, Eunsuk Bae*, Natasha
Ballack*, Joseph Bausano, Priya
Bhawsar, Eric Buck*, Max Carr, Lori
Chandler*, Lisa Cheung, Vikrant Dalvi,
Mike Damore*, Violette de la Selle,
Miwa Fukui, Guy Geier, Erica Godun,
Bhalchandra Gujar, Ji Ham, Cristina
Handal*, Brad Hartig*, William Haskas,
Carl Hauser, Jennifer Heiney*, Hector
Hinostroza*, Ervin Hirsan, Steven
Hong, Tony Hogge*, Dawn Hood,
Huan-Ting Hsiao, Carol Hsiung, Jill
Hughes, Daniel Jacoby, Jim Jirsa*,
Patrick Koch*, Blake Kurasek*, Heng-
Choong Leong, HK Li*, Erica Libritz,
Frank Lupo, Dean Mamalakis*,
Luciane Musso Maia, Brandon Massey,
Tim Milam, Christopher Musangi*,
Michael Nartey, Joseph Nocella,
Mark Nusbaum, Ung-Jib Park, Alvaro
Quintana, Gustavo Rodriguez, Alfreda
Radzicki, Roshan Raza, Gerald

Rosenfeld, Ananth Sampathkumar,
Paul Sanderson*, Andrew Shadid,
Bhumi Shah, Todd Shapiro*, Nicholas
Shrier, Gillian Sollenberger*, Julia
Spector, Timothy Sudweeks, Gerardo
Sustaeta, Maria Szmit*, Kristina
Tetkowski, Sebastian Touzet, Michael
Valenti, Edward Wagner, Raymond
Williams, Charles Wood, Bill Wagner*
*Epstein staff

Architect: FXFOWLE EPSTEIN
Construction Manager: Tishman
Construction, an AECOM Company
MEP Engineer: WSP Flack + Kurtz, Inc.
Structural Engineer: Leslie E.
Robertson & Associates
Structural Engineer of Record:
Weidlinger Associates
Site, Civil, Geotechnical Engineer:
Langan Engineering, Environmental,
Surveying and Landscape
Architecture, D.P.C.
Landscape Architect:
Ken Smith Landscape Architect
Lighting: Fisher Marantz Stone, Inc.
Daylighting: Carpenter
Norris Consulting, Inc.
Exterior Wall:
R. A. Heintges & Associates
Exterior Maintenance:
Entek Engineering PLLC
Roofing: Commercial
Roofing Solutions, Inc.
Concrete: Building Conservation
Associates, Inc.
Food Service: William
Caruso & Associates
Code, Life Safety, ADA Accessibility:
Rolf Jensen & Associates
Blast Analysis, Perimeter Security:
Weidlinger Associates
Telecommunications: HBR Consulting
Security: Kroll Schiff
Acoustics, A/V: Shen Milsom & Wilke, Inc.
Associate Architects: RCGA, EPoc
Partnership, Anthony C. Baker
Associate Engineers: Epstein

(Structural and MEP), Primera
Engineering (MEP)
Signage and Graphics:
Catt Lyon Design Incorporated
Traffic: Sam Schwartz Engineering, PLLC
Vertical Transportation: VDA Van
Deusen & Associates
LEED: Viridian Energy & Environmental
Specifications:
Construction Specifications, Inc.
Cost Estimating: Toscano Clements Taylor
Media Consulting: Tim Hunter Design
Hardware: Glezen Fisher Group LLC
Permit Expediter: JAM Consultants
Photography: Chris Cooper (p53,
60, 62), David Sundberg/Esto (p56,
58 lower, 59), Coe Hoeksema (57),
historic renderings courtesy of Pei
Cobb Freed & Partners Architects LLP,
construction photography courtesy of
Tishman Construction,
an AECOM Company

Water Street Redevelopment Vision Plan

Partner-in-Charge: Mark Strauss
Project Manager: Jason Hsiao
Project Designer: John Schuyler
Team: Toby Snyder

Landscape Architect: Starr Whitehouse
Landscape Architects and Planners
Traffic Engineer:
Sam Schwartz Engineering
Special Event Planning:
Karin Bacon Events
Real Estate Adviser: JDF Realty
Lighting: L'Observatoire International
Environmental Design: Sylvia Harris

Published by
ORO Editions
Publisher: Gordon Goff
Copyright © 2014 by FXFOWLE Architects, LLP
ISBN: 978-1-935935-63-6
10 09 08 07 06 5 4 3 2 1 First Edition

Consulting Editor: Andrea Monfried
Text: Liz Campbell Kelly
Design: ORO Editions
FXFOWLE Monograph Team: Guy Geier, Amanda Abel, Karen Bookatz, and Brien McDaniel
Color Separations and Printing: ORO Group Ltd.
Production: Usana Shadday and Alexandria Nazar
Printed in China

This book was printed and bound using a variety of sustainable manufacturing processes and materials including aqueous-based varnish, VOC- and formaldehyde-free glues, and phthalate-free laminations. The text is printed using offset sheetfed lithographic printing process in 5 color on 140 gsm woodfree art paper and 157 gsm matt art paper with an off-line spot gloss varnish applied to all photographs.

ORO Editions makes a continuous effort to minimize the overall carbon footprint of its publications. As part of this goal, ORO Editions, in association with Global ReLeaf, arranges to plant trees to replace those used in the manufacturing of the paper produced for its books. Global ReLeaf is an international campaign run by American Forests, one of the world's oldest nonprofit conservation organizations. Global ReLeaf is American Forests' education and action program that helps individuals, organizations, agencies, and corporations improve the local and global environment by planting and caring for trees.

Library of Congress Cataloging-in-Publication Data:
Available upon request